In loving memory of
Diana Rose Woerner
Samuel's "Nana"
June 8, 1956 – September 25, 2010

AuthorHouse™
1663 Liberty Drive
Bloomington, IN 47403
www.authorhouse.com
Phone: 1-800-839-8640

Published by AuthorHouse 06/18/2014

ISBN: 978-1-4969-1034-9 (sc)
ISBN: 978-1-4969-1035-6 (e)

Library of Congress Control Number: 2014908189

All scriptures were taken from the New King James Version of the bible unless otherwise designated
with (LB) which means those scriptures were taken from the Living Bible.

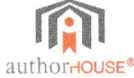

Samuel and His Nine Fine Furry Friends

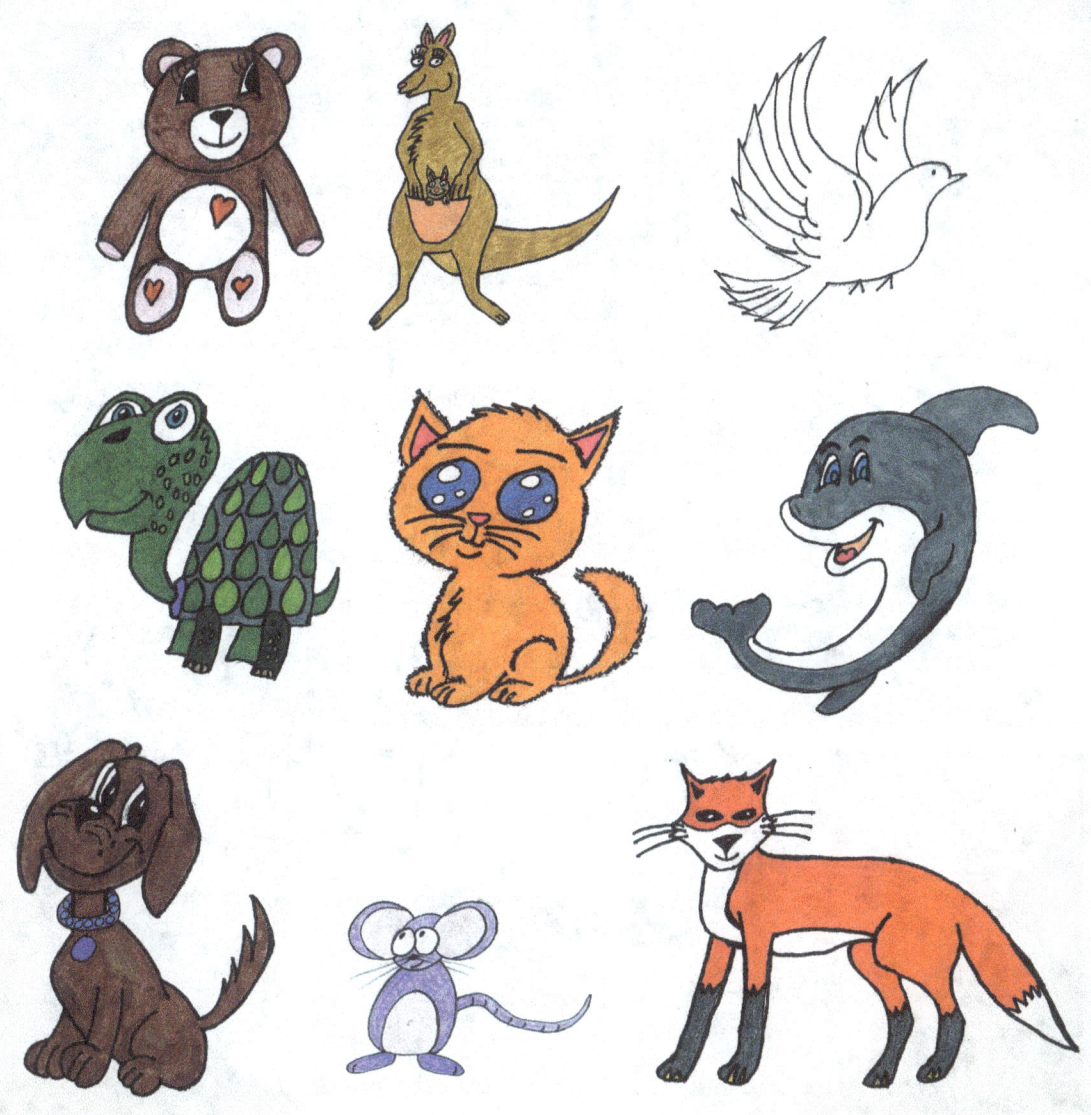

Carletta Sherrill Woerner

Animal illustrations by Dana Sherrill Bates

Other illustrations by Floyd Yamyamin

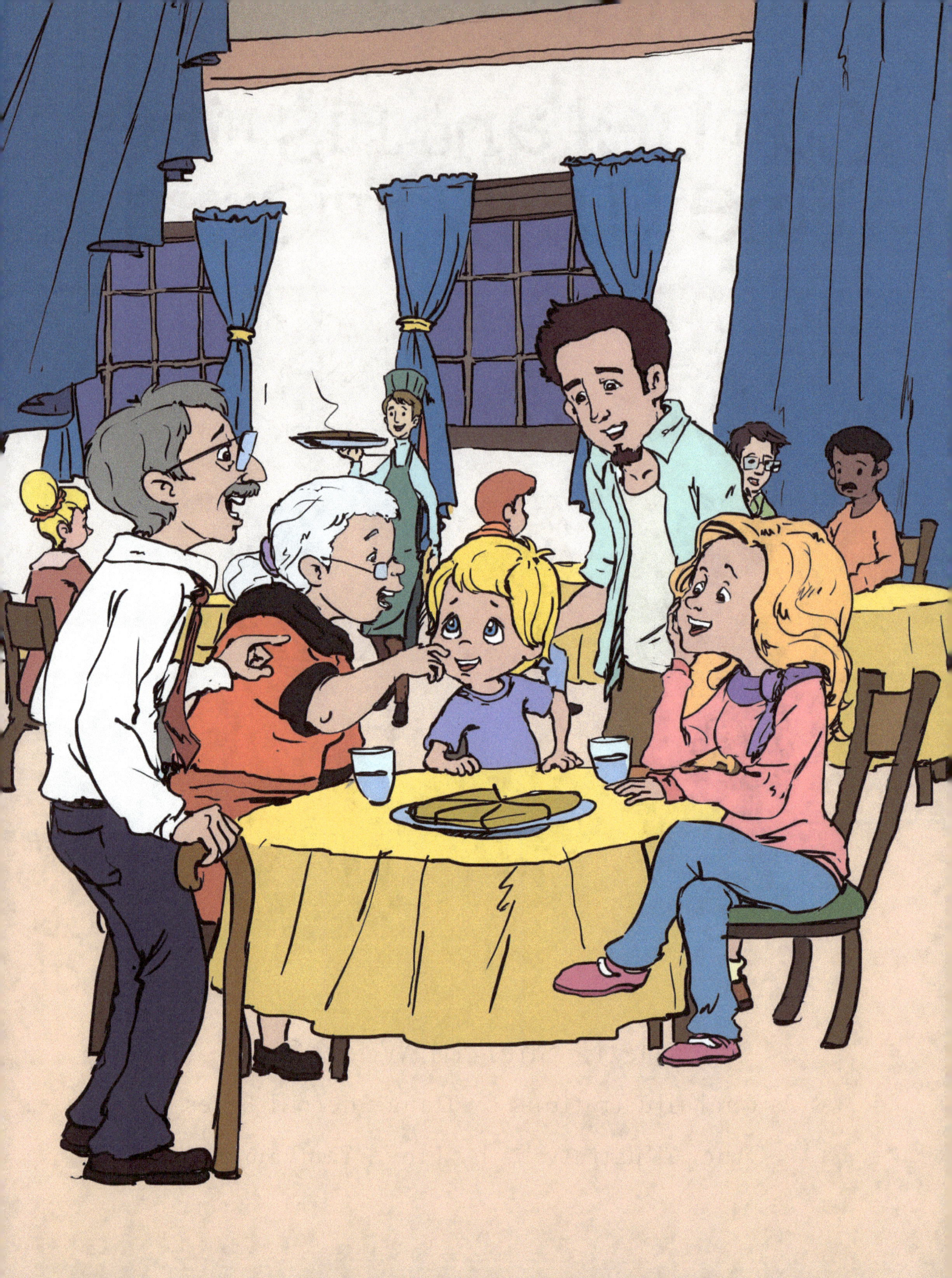

Once upon a time, there was a little boy named Samuel who had big blue eyes, blonde hair, and fair skin that was soft as silk. His cheeks were kiss-ably plump and his eyes sparkled when he smiled.

Everywhere Samuel went; people would stop his parents to declare, "What a handsome boy you have there." Not only was he a cute child but he was also a very good and happy boy.

He seemed to make others happy too. There was just something special about Samuel. He had a sweet spirit and seemed perfect in every way.

As for God, His way is perfect; The word of the Lord is proven… 2Samuel22:31

Samuel's parents, Amanda and Tom, wanted him to know and live God's word from an early age and to learn good values. So one day his parents decided to paint the words, **love, joy, peace, patience, kindness, goodness, faithfulness, gentleness and self control** on Samuel's blue walls in his bedroom. Next to each word was a stuffed animal to help him remember the fruits of the spirit that are found in the bible from Galatians 5:22.

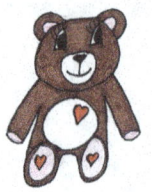

Love was a brown soft bear with a red heart on his chest.

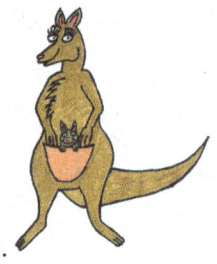

Joy was a kangaroo.

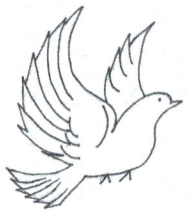

Peace was a white dove.

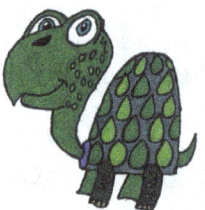

Patience was a green turtle.

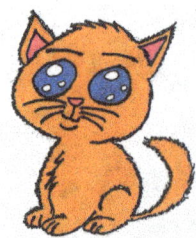

Kindness was an orange kitten.

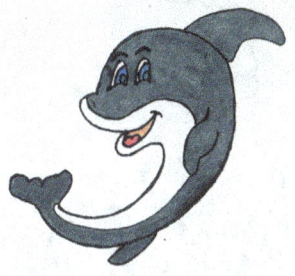

Goodness was a grey dolphin.

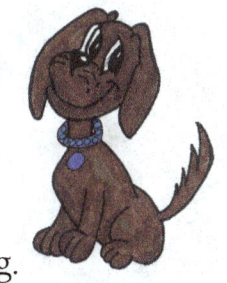

Faithfulness was a brown hairy dog.

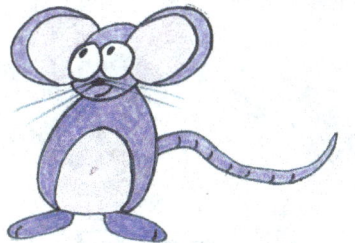

Gentleness was a tiny little mouse   and

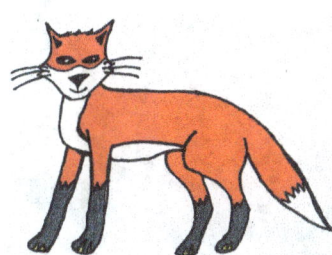

Self Control was a clever looking fox.

When Samuel's parents would tuck him in bed at night, they would teach him about these virtues and how important they are to living a good life. They would talk about God's great love for us and how we are to love Him and others as ourselves.

**And you must think constantly about these commandments
I am giving you today.
You must teach them to your children
and talk about them when you are at home
or out for a walk; at bedtime and the first thing in the morning.
Deuteronomy 6:6-7**

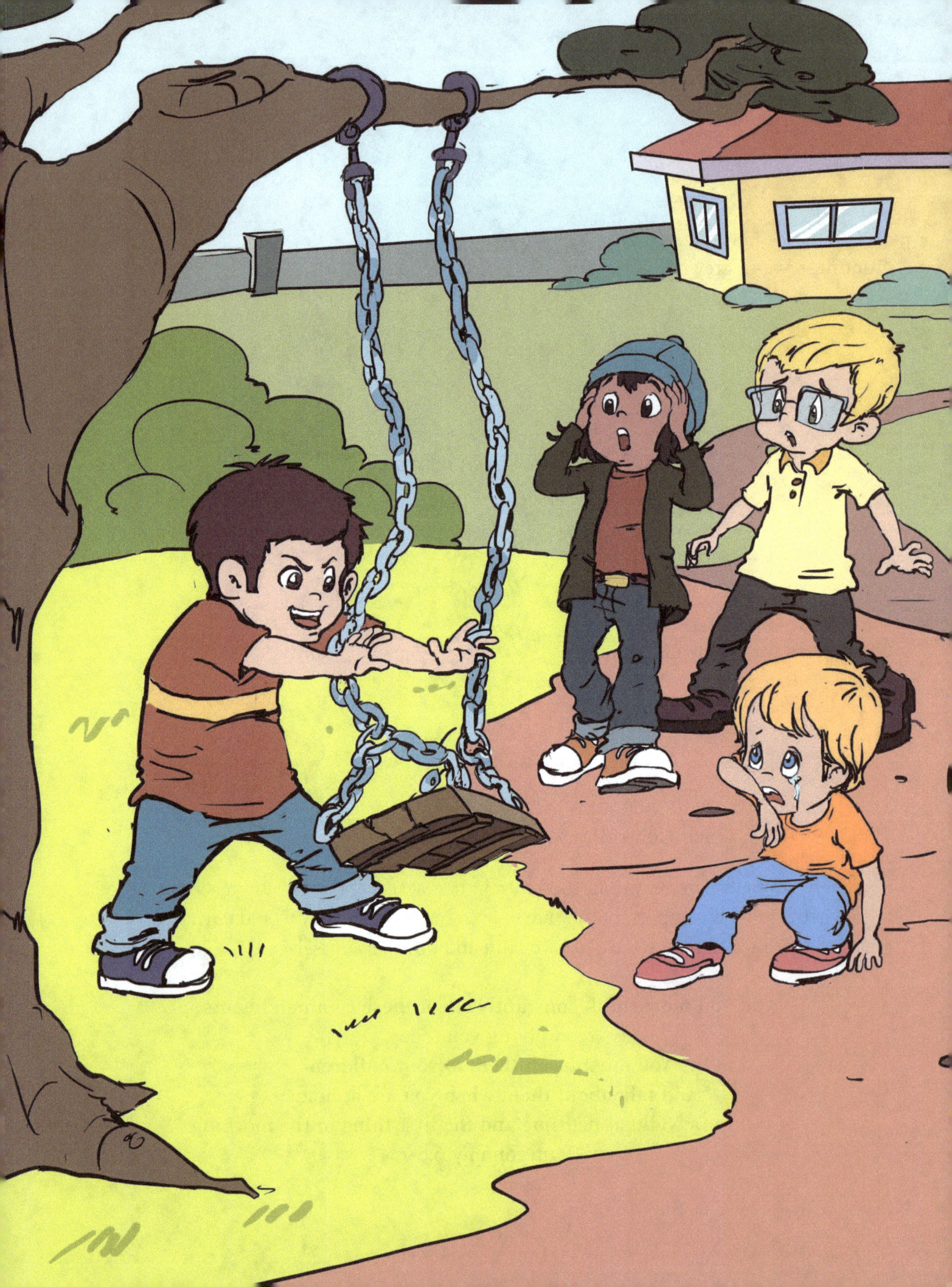

One day at school, a big boy named Joey, who was the class bully, hit Samuel and pushed him off the swings. Samuel's face was red with anger and embarrassment; tears were streaming down his chubby cheeks.

He picked himself up and was getting ready to push Joey, when he could almost

hear his mom say, "The **Love** bear   wants you to love everyone, as Christ loves

us. Be **patient** like green turtle.   Be Kind like **Kind** Kitten.   Be

Gentle   and do **Good**   to everyone even those who hurt you."

Just then, Samuel looked up and saw a white bird   sitting on a limb in the big tree in the playground. He felt a calm come over him, and he didn't want to be mean

to Joey anymore. He thought; this must be the **Peace**   my parents explained to me.

You will keep him in perfect peace,
whose mind is stayed on you. Isaiah 26:3

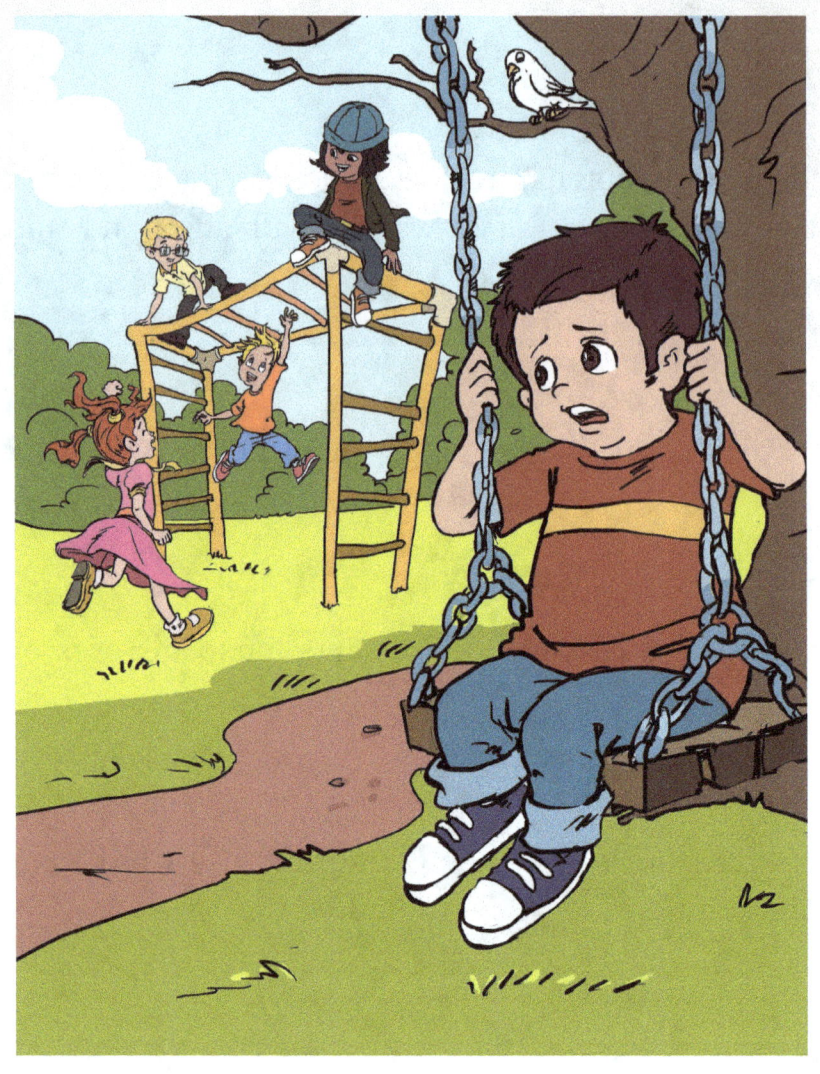

So instead of pushing the bully back, Samuel said, "Joey that wasn't nice, you shouldn't push people. If you would have asked me for the swing, I would have given it to you." Samuel turned and ran off to play on the jungle gym with some other children.

He felt happier, stronger and full of **joy**, because he knew God was

helping him practice **patience** and **self control**.

My strength is made perfect in weakness. 2Corinthians 12:9

Samuel's dad heard about the incident in the playground, when he came to pick Samuel up after school. He was so proud of his son. His dad smiled and thanked God for Samuel's sweet spirit and godly character. He squeezed Samuel <u>so</u>, <u>so</u> tightly and then gave him a fist bump.

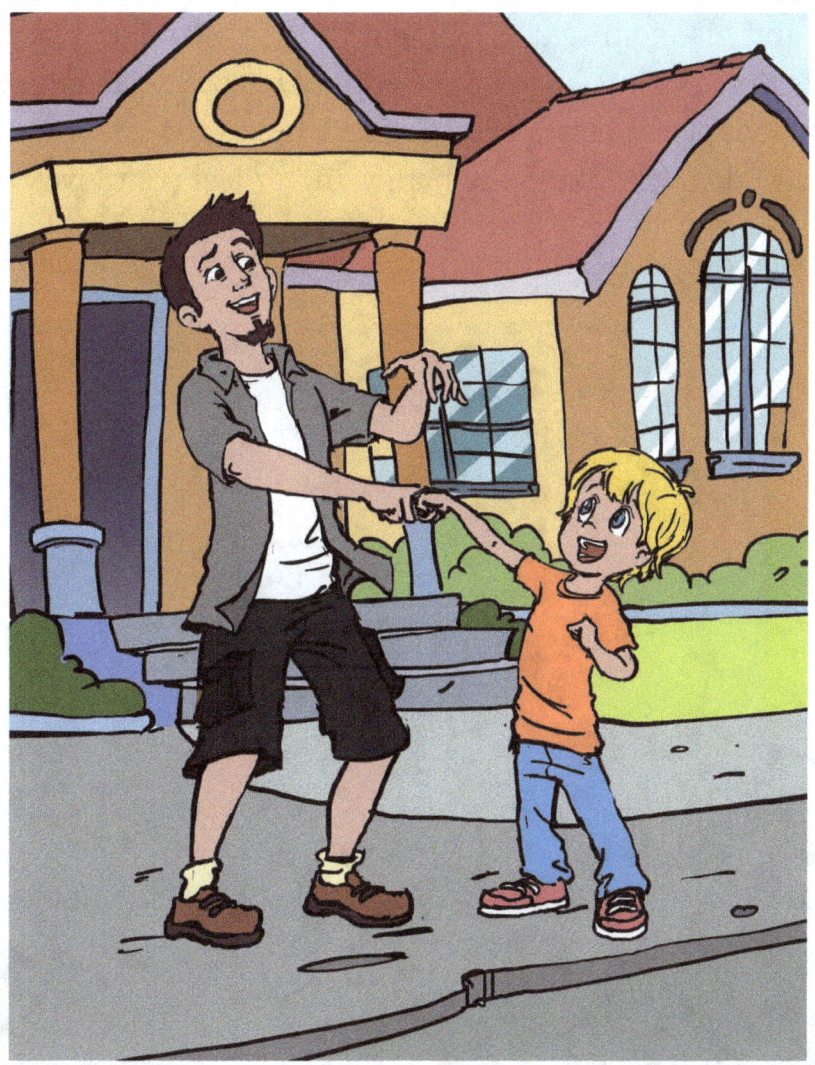

Happy is the man with a level-headed son…Proverbs 10:1 (LB)

Samuel knew his dad was proud of him and that gave him <u>great</u>, <u>great</u> **joy.** He knew, now, what the **Joy** Kangaroo represents. It wasn't just about being happy on the outside but it was about having a great big smile deep inside of him that made him feel good.

Even though Samuel was pleased with the way he treated Joey, he felt sad for him. He

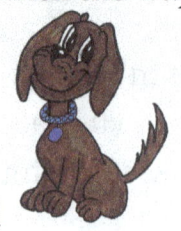

knew Joey didn't have many **faithful** friends and he felt sorry for him.

When Samuel and his mom said their night time prayers, he prayed a special prayer just for Joey. He got down on his knees at the edge of his bed, folded his sweet little hands and prayed, "Dear God, please help Joey to be good and to come to know you and my nine fine furry friends as I do. Help him to be happy and to feel your love."

Do not be overcome by evil, but overcome evil with good. Romans 12:21

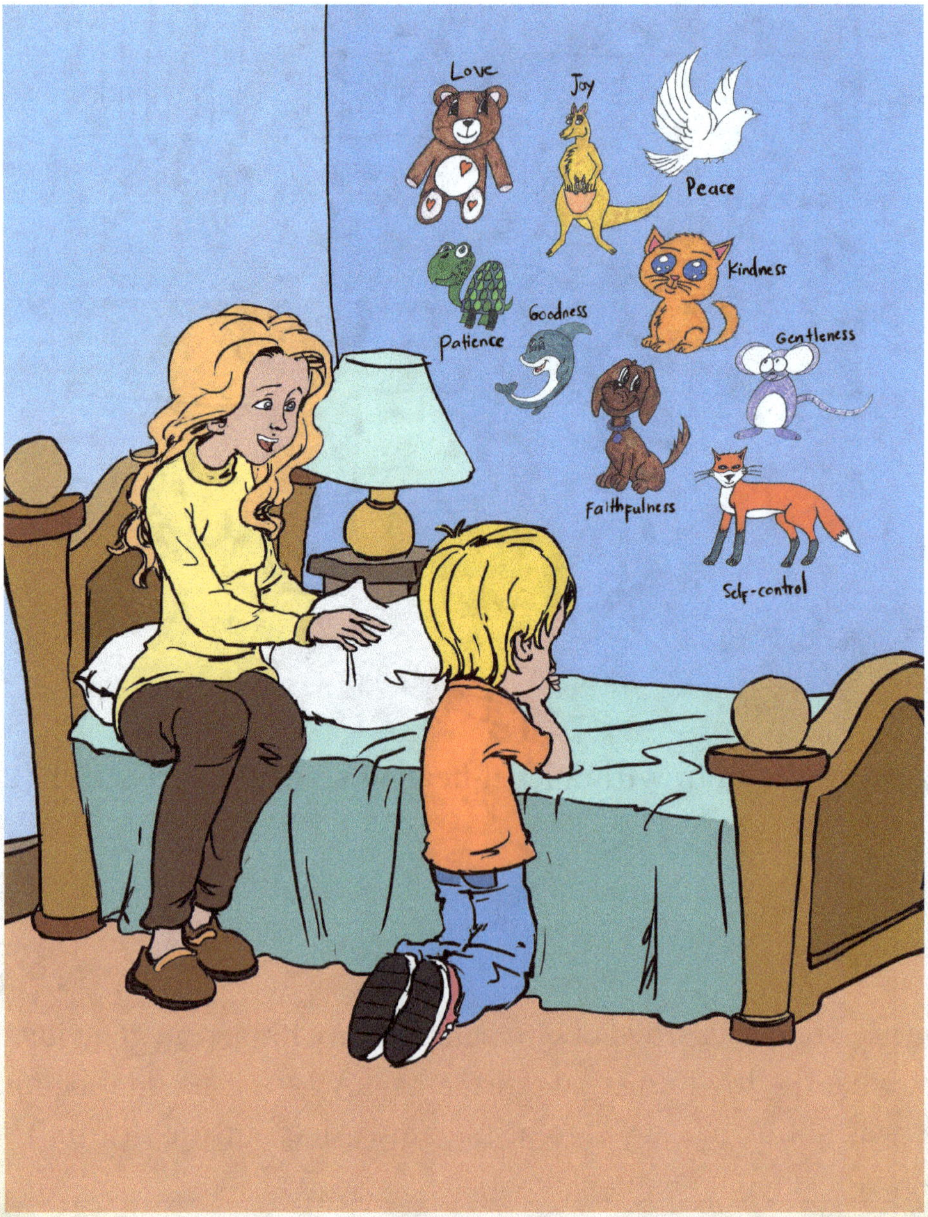

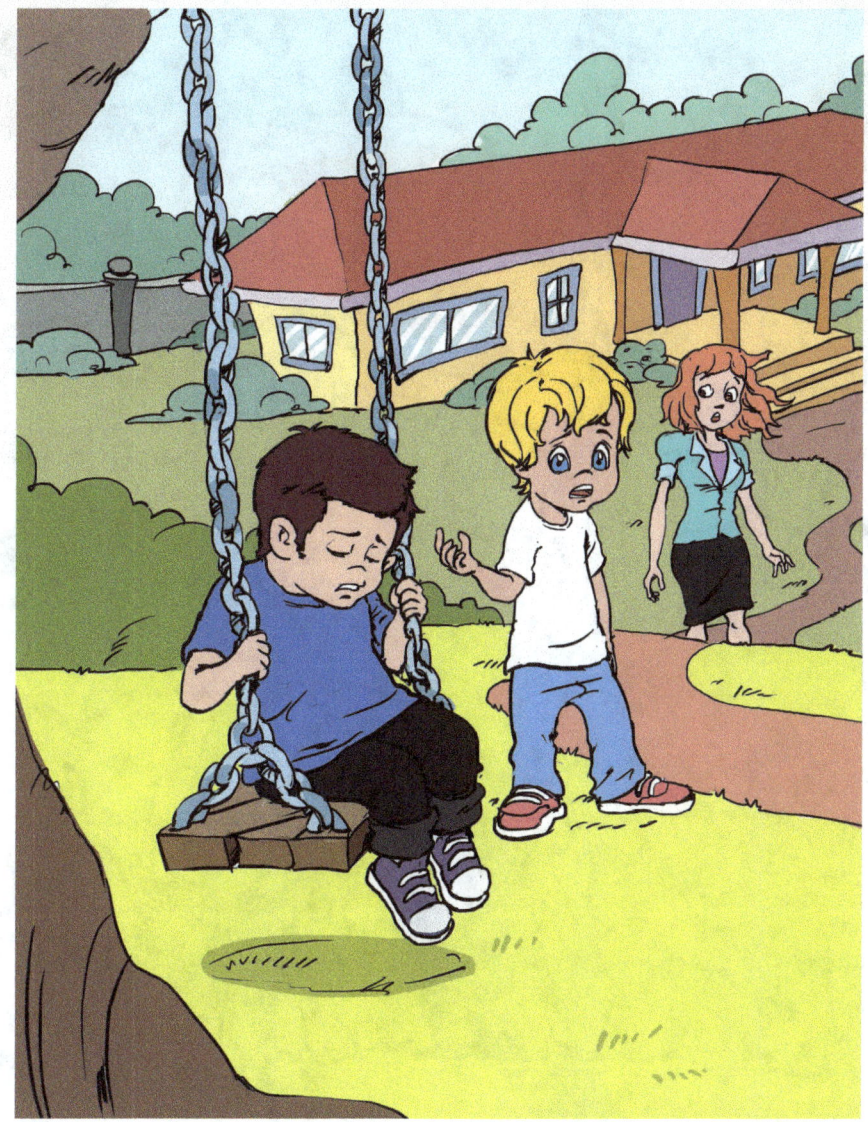

When Samuel got to school the next day, he saw Joey sitting alone on the swing and heard him sobbing. Samuel walked over and asked "Are you ok?" Joey tried to sound tough wiping the tears from his red cheeks and said in a quivering voice, "Yeh, I'm fine." Samuel said, "Why are you crying then?"

With that Joey cried harder and said, when I woke up this morning my daddy told me he was leaving and that he wasn't <u>ever</u>, <u>ever</u> coming back.

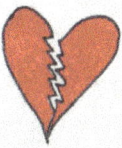

He said he loves me, but that he had to go.

The Lord is near to those who have a broken heart. Psalms 34:18

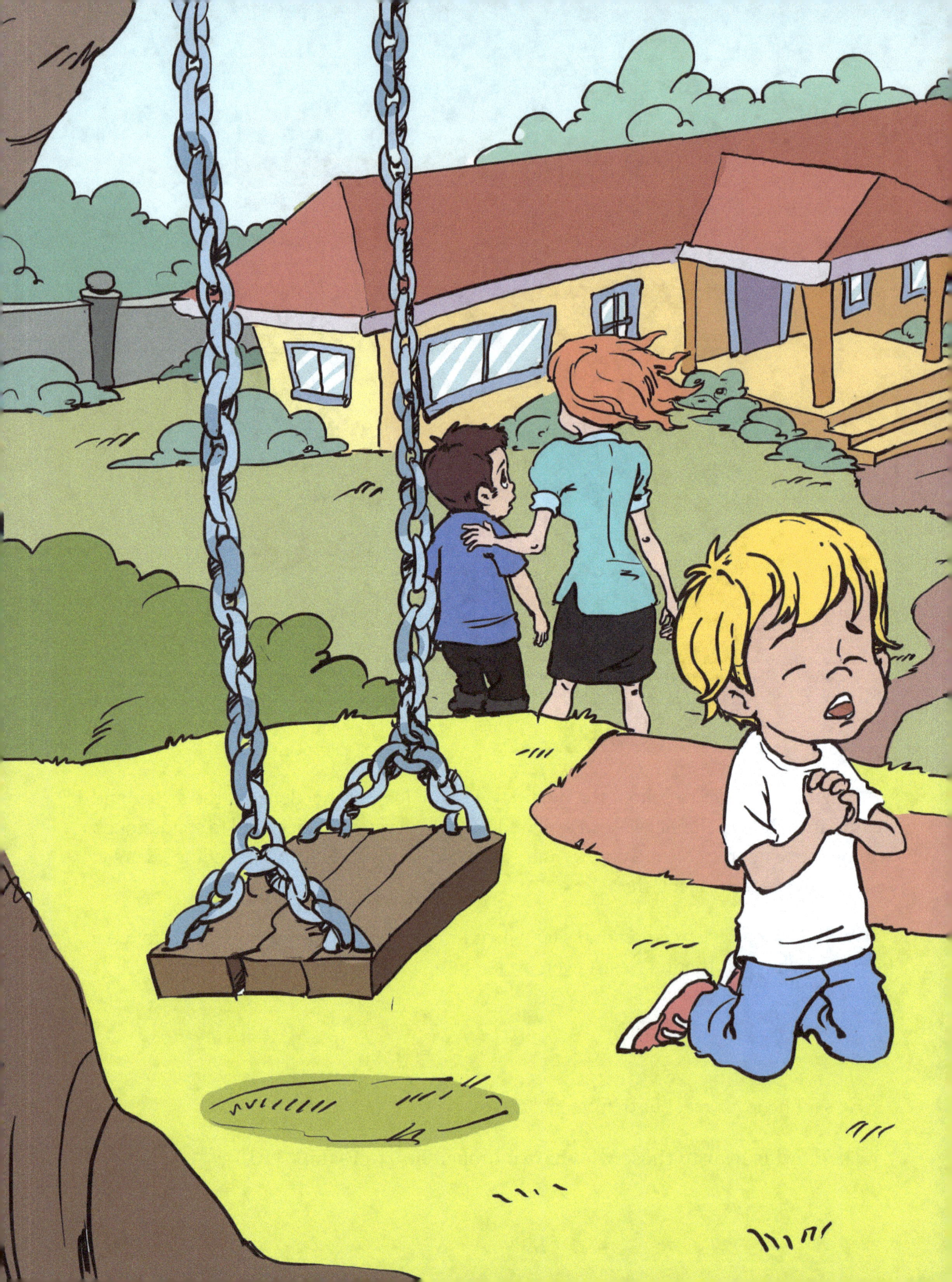

Then Joey cried <u>harder</u> and <u>harder.</u> The teacher came over and gave Joey a hug and walked him into the school. Samuel cried too. He felt so sad as if his little heart was

breaking for Joey. He was feeling compassion and had a gentle   spirit for Joey. Samuel never felt that feeling before and he knew he wanted to help Joey in some way. Samuel prayed right there in the school yard, "God show me how to help Joey. What can a little kid like me do to make him feel better?"

Suddenly, he thought about his nine fine furry friends hanging on his walls and knew how important it is to share their message with Joey and be his friend. If Joey ever needed a friend, he needed one now. Samuel remembered a scripture that his parents taught him that said,

A friend loves at all times. Proverbs 17:17

Samuel knew God had answered his prayer. He was determined to do what he could to become a friend to Joey. At lunch time, Samuel shared his sandwich with Joey, since he forgot his that morning. The boys began walking home together and Joey would come over to Samuel's house after school when he could. They would play ball in the back yard and even do homework together. Joey seemed to do better in school and was much happier, but he missed his dad <u>so</u> much. Samuel eventually, told Joey about his nine fine furry friends and about God's great love for him.

One day Samuel and his mom went to visit Joey and his mother. Amanda made one of her famous cherry pies to give them and Samuel brought a special gift for Joey.

Amanda and Joey's mom sat in the living room talking about God's love and how he provides for His children. While the boys were in Joey's room strategically placing stuffed animals on his book shelves. Samuel purchased a set of nine fine furry friends to give Joey for his room and a children's bible. He read from Galatians 5:22 and explained how each one of these stuffed animals helped him remember the fruits of the spirit and to live by them.

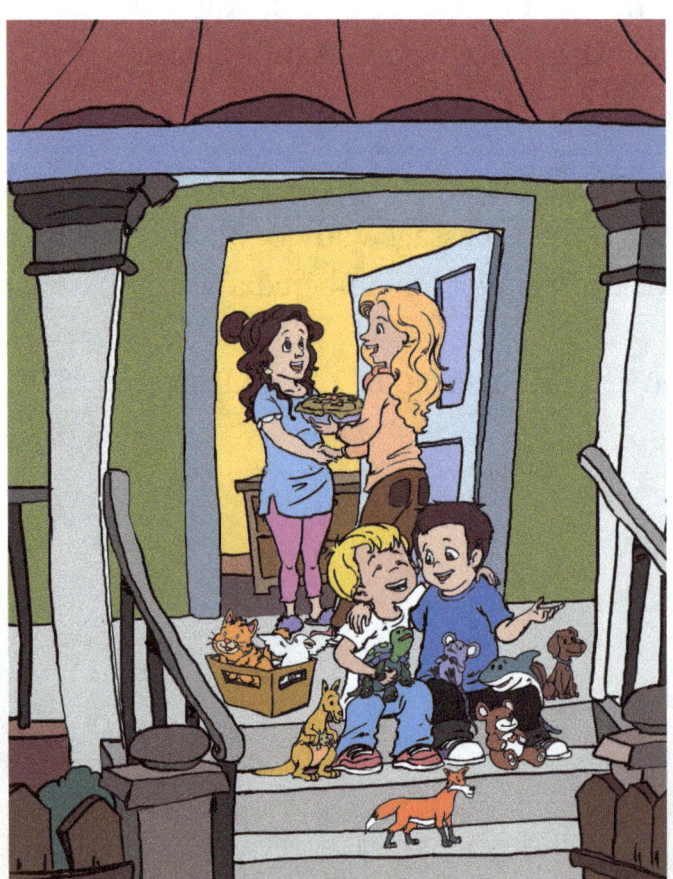

But certainly God has heard me; He has attended to the voice of my prayer.
Psalm 66:19-20

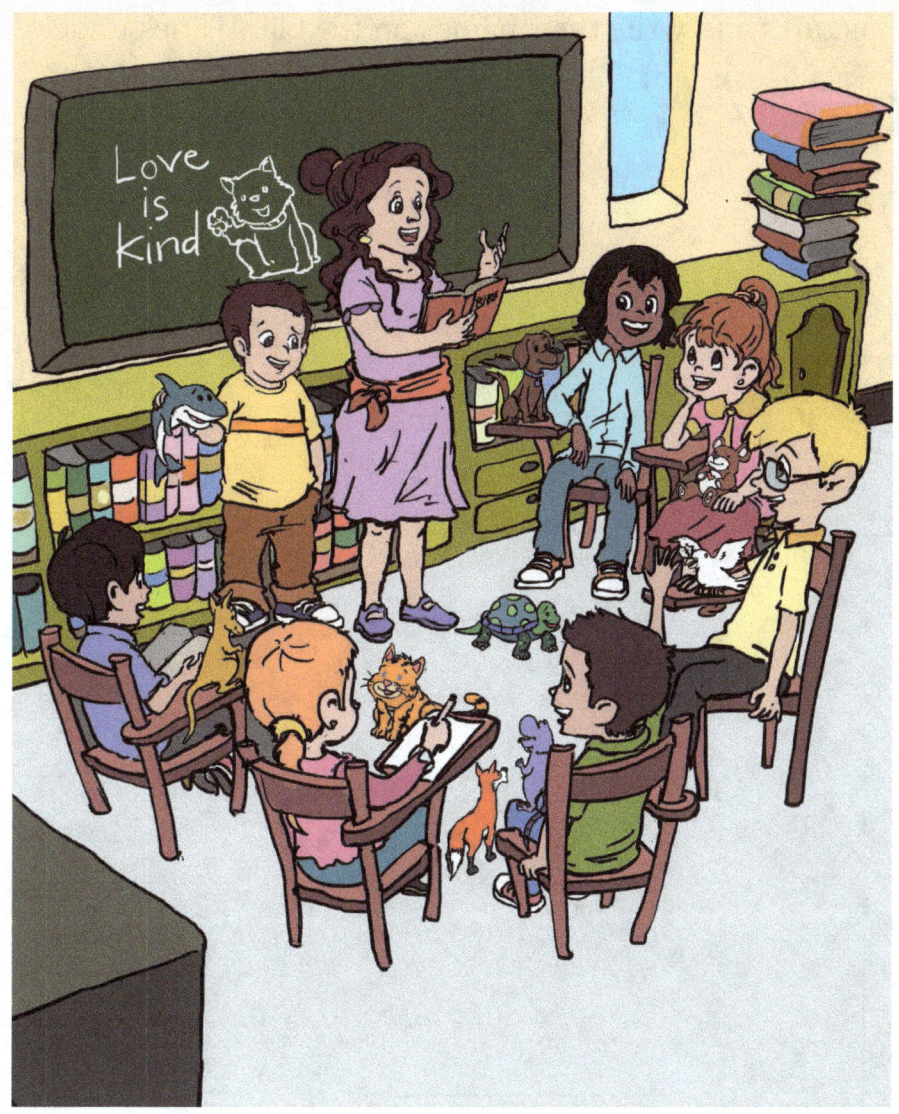

Joey and his mom started to attend the same church where Samuel and his family worshipped. The two families became good friends and spent quality time together. Joey and his mom developed many close friendships and became involved in the children's ministry at the church.

Samuel's friendship and his compassionate spirit made a life changing influence on two people. Now they are touching the hearts and lives of many more families by their desire to share the love and message of Jesus Christ.

And I pray that as you share your faith with others it will grip their lives too, as they see the wealth of good things in you that come from Christ Jesus.
Philemon 1:6 (LB)

The end…

Color in the pictures and write their names on the blank lines under each animal.

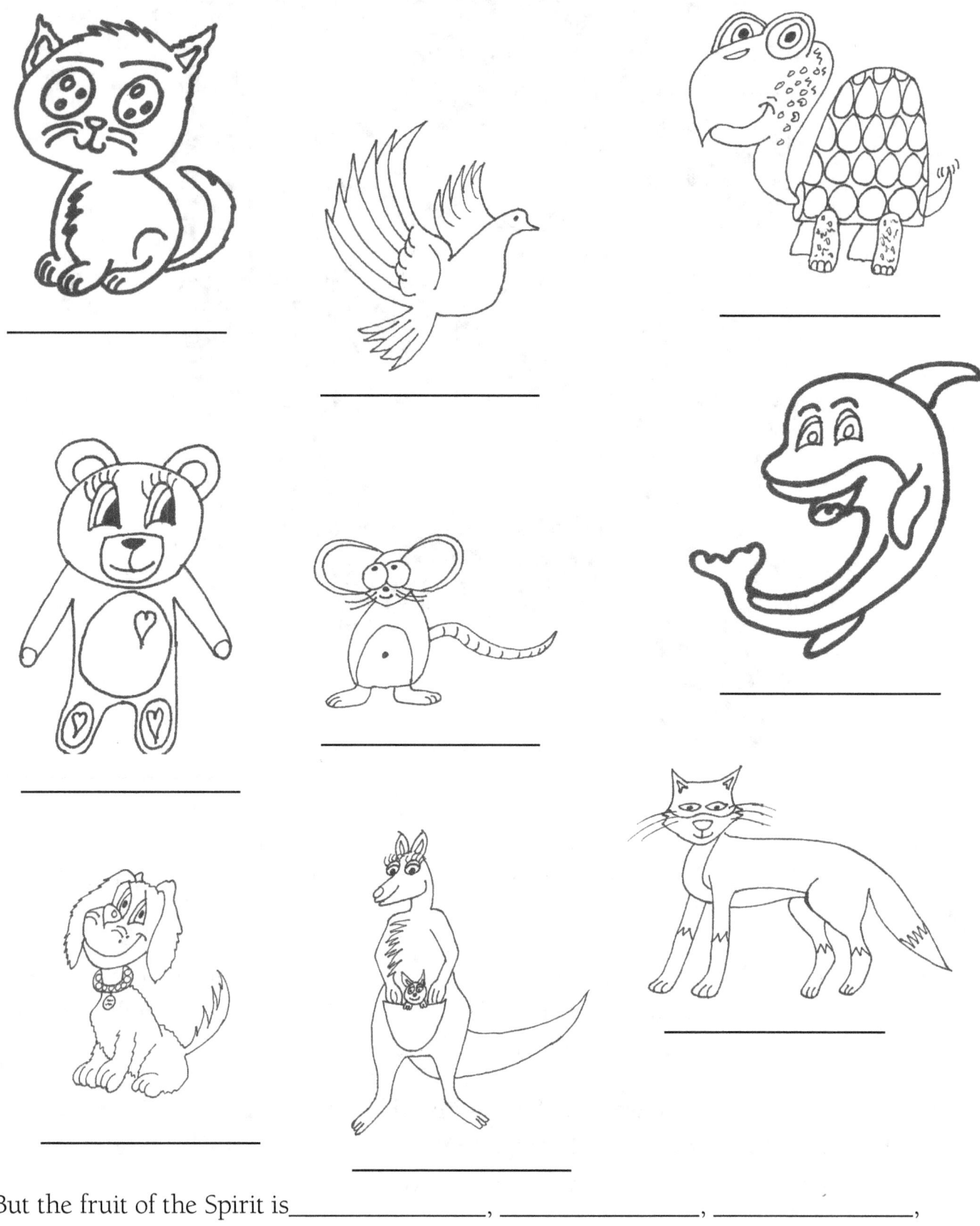

_____

_____

_____

_____

_____

_____

_____

_____

_____

But the fruit of the Spirit is_____, _____, _____, _____, _____, _____, _____, _____, _____.

Dear God,

Help me to live as you want me to live. Show me how to LOVE everyone even those who are not kind to me. Help me to have JOY and PEACE even when I am having a tough day and things aren't going my way. Give me Patience when I want something and think I need it right now. Teach me to have Kindness, GOOdness, Faithfulness and Gentleness to all, big and small. Train me to have Self Control every day in all my ways. Amen

www.ingramcontent.com/pod-product-compliance
Lightning Source LLC
Chambersburg PA
CBHW081826170526
45167CB00008B/3558